Good Trouble

A Shoeleather History of Nonviolent Direct Action

by
Steve Thornton

HARDBALL

PRESS

RAVES FOR *GOOD TROUBLE*!

...Great little book! I'm with you, all the way, and especially now. I don't think there has ever been a time in American history when we have so needed good trouble.
—Frances Fox Piven, *Challenging Authority:*
How Ordinary People Change America

Drawn from Thornton's Shoeleather History people's history project of Hartford, *Good Trouble* is much more than a valuable local history. Coupled with Thornton's thoughtful introduction, these clearly-written sketches are tales of creativity, courage, and social justice activism by ordinary people who take on politicians, bosses, slumlords, and bigots.
—Dexter Arnold, *New Hampshire Labor News*

This history, in the tradition of Howard Zinn, tells the story of change from the perspective of people in the streets rather than from the gilded walls of corporate, or Washington, offices.
—Jackie Allen-Doucot,
St. Martin De Porres Catholic Worker

The 'disruptive' actions Thornton mentions are not intended to be isolated events or substitutes for other organizing. Rather, they usually represent 'moments' playing contributing (sometimes crucial) roles in ongoing struggles.
—Nick Braune, South Texas College

Steve Thornton is a retired union organizer who has spent forty-five years on the front lines of student, labor, community, environmental, and anti-racist struggles.

—*Labor World* **(Duluth, MN)**

When Thornton says nonviolent direct action is a great antidote to despair, he's speaking from his experience as a union organizer, nonviolent action trainer, and as a participant in many of the stories he chronicles....

—**Arnie Alpert,** *InZane Times*

If you live in Hartford and call yourself an activist, then you owe it to yourself to read Steve Thornton's latest book... Its digestible nuggets help good troublemakers place themselves within the context of a larger narrative.

—**Kerri Provost,** *Real Hartford*

This book comes to us at a time when faith in our democracy is fading. We need to revisit the stories of those who do not give up even when all of the odds are against them.

—**Rev. Damaris Whittaker,**
Senior Minister, Ft. Washington Collegiate Church NY

Library of Congress Cataloging-in-Publication Data:
Thornton, Steve
Good Trouble, A Shoeleather History of Nonviolent
Direct Action

The information in this book is true and complete
to the best of our knowledge. It is offered without
guarantee on the part of the author or Hardball Press.
The author and Hardball Press disclaim all liability in
connection with the use of this book.

On the cover: 'John Lewis: Good Trouble' by Eric Millikin
Cover & book design by D. Bass
Set in Palatino Lino.
Published by Hard Ball Press, Brooklyn, New York
ISBN: 978-1-7328088-7-4
www.hardballpress.com

Contents

Introduction   1

Community/Neighborhood   7

River of Tears   7

Invasion of the Rat Catchers   8

Ray Adams Stands His Ground   9

No Vacancy: Families Fight for Housing   12

"We are Connecticut Refugees"   14

City Hall Paint Job   13

The Trucks Stop Here   16

Linkage Blockade   18

Protest Camp at the Library:

       Mark Twain Would Approve   20

Work/Labor   **23**

"We Irish Are a Working Race."   23

Factory Girls Strike for Their Health   25

"Something to Show for Our Work":

       The Unemployed Organize   27

The Gandhi Strike   30

The Colt 45: Peace Work with a Union Label   31

"They Treat the Worker Badly":

       Striking for Respect   35

Huelga de Brazos Caido: Justice for Janitors   37

Locked Out, Not Knocked Down   38

Moral Monday Turn Up   39

Civil Rights   **43**

Breaking the UPS Race Barrier   43

Turn Left or Be Shot   45

Poverty and Power Collide   46

The People's Legislature   47

Puerto Rican Youths Create a

     "Liberated Space"   49

Isabel Blake, Welfare Warrior   51

Anti-War   **55**

Anti-War Vets Take the Armory,

     Occupy a Church   55

Mining the Connecticut River   56

Women Beat Oppressive Grand Jury   57

Unwelcome Guests at Senator Dodd's Office 60

Vieques Supporters say "Ni Una Bomba Mas " 61

Tail Gunner Joe Can't Take the Heat   64

Human Rights   **67**

Inmates Strike at Seyms Street Jail   67

Gay Power, from Stonewall to Hartford   70

ADAPT Sledgehammers Make

     a Big Impression   71

The Squatters of People's Housing Action 73

Save Our Homeless People   76

Forty Days, One Million Dead 78

Smoking Out the Corporate Giant 79

Immigrants Welcome Here 81

Students **85**

Refusing to Hide from Nuclear War 85

Trinity College Sit-In Gets the Goods 86

Students Teach their Elders About Free Press 88

General Student Strike 91

Bibliography **95**

Good Writing on Nonviolent Direct Action 95

Books by Gene Sharp: 96

I Warned You: Books that argue against

Nonviolent Direct Action 96

About the Author **97**

Titles From Hard Ball Press **99**

For Matt, Megan, Pepper, and Kate

Introduction

Direct action is when ordinary people ignore the 'No Trespassing' sign and intervene directly on the stage of history. Small acts, when multiplied by millions of people, can transform the world.

--Howard Zinn

Here's the thing: nonviolent direct action and civil disobedience are frequently dismissed in activist circles as ineffective, or purely symbolic. Not a significant strategy for progressive social change. Over the course of past century, however, people in the city of Hartford, Connecticut have disproved this faulty analysis time and time again.

There is nothing wrong with symbolism, of course. Symbols have power. But ineffective action is a waste of our precious individual and collective energy; the challenge is to create potent tools for social change.

Another criticism of militant nonviolence is that only middle class white people can afford to use it. The stories in this book, however, demonstrate how nonviolent action has consistently been embraced by the city's working class African American and Puerto Rican communities.

As Alicia Garza, co-founder of Black Lives

Matter, has written: "Every successful social movement in the country's history has used disruption as a strategy to fight for social change."

Defining the term

That is why the stories in this collection are so important. In every case, these "people power" actions are undertaken by ordinary folks to make real changes in their lives. And they have. The results have been concrete, practical, and effective. They have contributed to local, national, and even international campaigns for economic, social, and racial justice.

Mass civil resistance actions are often illegal, but not always. In many cases the activists were well versed in nonviolence principles; other times they were completely spontaneous. (I recommend that if you plan to engage in such acts, find an experienced nonviolence trainer to help you prepare.) They came together to act, despite repercussions, because they found the "official channels" to be impotent, or worse, a trap.

For the purposes of this book, I define nonviolent direct action as a technique of struggle outside of institutional methods (laws, courts, petitions, voting) without the use of injurious force or threat to others. It is open and direct conflict that exposes oppression. It uses a set of special tactics that do not necessarily exclude coercion or property destruction. It is protest, resistance, or intervention to stop injustice and/or to win control over aspects of the political and economic life of our society.

The sociologists Frances Fox Piven and Richard

Cloward wrote that "the poor have few resources for regular political influence. Their ability to create social change depends on the disruptive power of tactics such as militant boycotts, sit-ins, traffic tie-ups, and rent strikes." Protest movements, they explained, gain real leverage by causing "commotion among bureaucrats, excitement in the media, dismay among influential segments of the community, and strain for political leaders."

Principles of Nonviolent Direct Action

Nonviolent direct action can be a very versatile tool in your organizing tool box. Here is a brief list of its practical applications. As you read the stories in this book, you will find that they fit one or more of these categories. Nonviolent direct action can:

-Directly stop an injustice;
-Assert or defend a positive right despite the consequences;
-Show willful refusal to cooperate with or participate in an injustice;
-Sound the alarm and alert folks to a problem;
-Amplify people's voices;
-Create a community-based solution.

The use of direct action shouldn't be seen as a "one off." It should be grounded in a vision, with goals, a strategy, and tactics. It can be part of an effective campaign that grows bigger, escalates, gains power, and wins.

Of course, not every use of nonviolence produces an instant victory, despite what you find in these pages. You can think of it as an essential component of movement-building.

When you and your cohorts engage in nonviolent direct action, you are likely to feel stronger and more self-confident, more autonomous, and less afraid. The "bystanders" who witness your action are also affected by it, even if it only makes them angry. When other people see you taking risks, it makes them ask "Why?"

As Dr. King wrote in *Letter from a Birmingham Jail*: "Nonviolent direct action seeks to create such a crisis and foster such a tension that a community which has constantly refused to negotiate is forced to confront the issue."

The stories here are categorized by topic, and within the topics, by chronology. At the end is a list of books and websites that provide much more information about people power.

I have also included a list of some books that attempt to discredit nonviolent direct action, so the reader can further explore the disagreements that have arisen over the years. Keep in mind that when the "violence vs. nonviolence" argument comes up, it can be an awful drain on your energy, more heat than light. A better topic to explore might be nonviolence vs. non-action.

You will notice that every story is written in the present tense. That's my attempt to bring these courageous acts to life, out from the dim past.

John Lewis, legendary civil rights organizer, led an unprecedented sit-in on the floor of the House of Representatives on June 22, 2016. "Dr. King and Rosa Parks inspired me to get in trouble. Good trouble," the veteran activist explained.

It is in the spirit of John Lewis, and of so many others from different eras, that this book is dedicated.

Steve Thornton
2019

Community/Neighborhood

River of Tears
May 14, 1969

Two young Hartford boys drown in the Park River in 1968. A parent group forms to demand that the river's depth be lowered to 1.5 feet. Now, a year later, the river is still 6 to 8 feet deep. Seven children have died here since the 1940s. "We have decided to get militant," says a protester. The parents are joined by local school teachers and the Black Panthers, including Butch Lewis, a Vietnam veteran who is under constant surveillance by the Federal Bureau of Investigation (FBI).

As they march down Flatbush Avenue, traffic backs up. The police arrive. "I sympathize," says Captain Pilon, "so why don't you do things like they should be done?"

"We did what we were supposed to-- for a year-- and got nothing," says Charter Oak Terrace tenant leader Barbara Henderson.

One car tries to force its way through the crowd. It is halted by protesters' bodies.

What none of the participants know is that they are being secretly observed by the FBI. Agents are writing urgent memos about community actions and sending them directly back to J. Edgar Hoover. The local bureau office classifies the Charter Oak Terrace protest as "Possible Racial Violence."

Butch Lewis, 2014
(Thornton)

The next day the concerned neighbors are back on the street. This time they announce an additional demand to the City: the bridge that spans the river is also a hazard and it needs to be fixed. By the end of the day, Public Works has fortified the structure.

Soon after the protests, the parents meet with Governor John Dempsey. He orders the removal of the downstream dams that have been keeping the water level artificially high.

The water recedes, the parents win, the children are safe.

Invasion of the Rat Catchers
September 16, 1975

The residents of Babcock Street have had it. The run-down two-family house nearby on Capitol Avenue is an eyesore and a health hazard. But what can be done about it?

The newly-organized Hartford Areas Rally Together (HART) takes a page from legendary Chicago community organizer Saul Alinsky. The group uncovers who the owner is and plans its strategy. They invite Doo Lee, the building's owner, to attend a neighborhood meeting about cleaning up the area. Lee does not attend.

Fortunately for the residents, their research also identifies Lee's business. He owns the South Seas restaurant in West Hartford. One autumn night, fifteen block club members show up at the eatery, walk into the restaurant with the signs, and leaflet the patrons.

This is a big step for these Hartford neighbors. They have never been involved in anything like this before. But they feel strongly about the blight, they are frustrated with bureaucratic inaction, and they trust each other.

Mr. Lee appears from his office to face the disrupters. They chide him for ignoring their meeting invitation, which they say is a sign of disrespect. They tell him (and the restaurant guests) about the rats that use his building as a safe haven. Lee blames the conditions on his tenants. They insist that Lee sign an agreement they have drawn up, promising that he will clean up the property.

He signs it and the clean up begins.

Ray Adams Stands His Ground
November 29, 1976

Snow and ice rain down on a small group crowded

in the doorway of 18 Congress Street. It's a one-way street between Wethersfield and Franklin Avenues where Hartford's south end begins. In the middle of the group is a young artist named Ray Adams, the building's last tenant.

The city inspector arrives to deliver an eviction notice. Ray's supporters continue to block the building's entrance. The inspector brings the police, but the protesters bring the TV cameras. The officials back off.

Ray Adams has begun the public fight for affordable housing in Hartford. It's a campaign opposed to the "gentrification" scheme which replaces low-income and working families with upper

Blocking the eviction notice
(courtesy of Homefront archives)

income residents. Officials hope this influx will shore up the City's shrinking tax base.

These wealthy tenants-- who have any number of other housing options already-- are dubbed "urban pioneers." "It's a class issue," Ray says.

For nine months, Ray Adams has been living at 18 Congress Street without heat or hot water. He is the last of 800 families who had been living in the four-block Charter Oak-South Green development area, some of them for as long as 35 years. When the properties were bought by the City of Hartford and handed over to a private developer, living conditions rapidly deteriorated through neglect, vandalism, and, the tenants suspect, sabotage.

A City Council leader announces that Ray would have first dibs on a new apartment– as long as he can come up with the rent. The holdout tenant replies that he has no intention of moving *back* into the neighborhood because, he says, "I don't intend to *leave*."

Ray Adams has become a community celebrity. He uses his fame to visit other apartment renters who are fighting evictions or landlord neglect. Hartford tenants are organizing for more control over their housing conditions, frequently raising the slogan "People before Profit."

Not everyone agrees with the fair housing advocates. The Hartford Architecture Conservancy (HAC) is singularly unsympathetic to Ray. "There is no point in crying over the way things might have been," the group writes in its newsletter. Ray's fight starts a backlash against HAC. Its "At Home In Hartford" tour for suburbanites is met with a tenant march through city streets. HAC then ends the annual event.

Six months after the failed eviction, city officials take Ray and his supporters by surprise and successfully kick him out of his apartment. They threaten to break down his door with a sledge-hammer and axe and throw his belongings into the street. But Ray's fight has defined the way Hartford looks at "urban renewal" and the housing crisis in a way that has not been done before.

After the Congress Street battle, community groups step up their opposition to gentrification. They argue for rent control and the protection of existing housing stock from private developers who are tearing down apartment units. They organize against tax breaks for new downtown office buildings. They fight for and win the Housing Preservation and Replacement ordinance, a groundbreaking law that makes developers provide new housing when their high-rises destroy existing homes.

When you ride down Congress Street today, look for the Berwick building, built in 1913. That's where Ray Adams and his friends took their stand.

No Vacancy: Families Fight for Housing
November 12, 1980

Homeless families, led by the Neighborhood Housing Coalition, organize a sit-in at Hartford City Hall. The action is spurred by the city's housing crisis, where affordable housing is so scarce that the vacancy rate is less than one percent. "The City Council has sat around enough...and done very little for the people who live and sweat and die in this city," says Antonio Soto of La Casa de Puerto Rico.

The City Council largely ignores the action, and one member, Robert Ludgin, calls protesters' demand for decent housing "absurd." The activists want some of Hartford's $3.3 million budget surplus to be used to finance new housing and to repair existing housing stock. They also want the City to press harder for 200 units of public housing promised by HUD but later revoked.

The sit-in lasts two days until the occupiers negotiate a plan to move to the Hartford Hilton (located on Bushnell Park) which is empty and undergoing renovation. City officials pledge that the families can stay at the Hilton until they find permanent housing.

About 50 people stay at the hotel for two weeks until city officials call for them to leave. A judge blocks the eviction after legal advocates charge that the Hilton's owners – Travelers' Insurance, Aetna, and developer David Chase – have acted illegally in their attempt to evict the families. At the court hearing, Carmen Luciano tells how she has lived in Hartford for 20 years and only lost her apartment after tending to a sick relative in Puerto Rico. "The only place I have left is the streets, nothing else," she tells the judge.

One week later, after pressure mounts from the business community, the same judge orders the tenants out. On December 1st, more than 100 people join the families in a march in front of the hotel. Within days, the families are relocated, some to a different hotel and others to permanent housing.

"We are Connecticut Refugees"
March 18, 1981

Eleven homeless families-- black and white, young

and old-- take their protest to the State Capitol. They have been kicked out of their temporary lodgings, a Wethersfield motel. "I've been in motels, I've been at the Salvation Army," says Barbara Crabbe, one of the protestors. "I've put my kids in foster homes to try and get on my feet. But I'm trapped."

Tenants fight for their homes on Huyshope Avenue
(Nick Lacy)

City officials say they are unable to find alternative housing for the families. Now the homeless mothers are angry and ready to risk arrest. They bring all their possessions to the Capitol, carried in plastic bags.

"If I've got to be arrested every night to get a roof over my head, okay," says Barbara Crabbe. "What can we do?" responds the agency administrator, who admits there is simply no budget for adequate housing.

The families are forced to leave the Capitol, so

they move to the state welfare office. Two of the women refuse to leave and are arrested. "We are Connecticut refugees," says Doris Lewison as she is being led into the police van.

State officials promise all the families will have permanent housing by the end of the week, but it does not materialize. Unwilling to give up, the welfare moms move back to the Capitol briefly before being evicted once again.

The families end up at Sacred Heart Church -- along with Salvadoran families who have fled their government's state-sanctioned violence. The two groups bond, and the local El Salvador support group provides the welfare moms with food.

After two weeks of constant struggle, the families receive permanent housing at the Dutch Point public housing project.

City Hall Paint Job
1984

Hartford Areas Rally Together (HART) is the city's oldest community organizing group. HART announces it will move into City Hall, demanding a six-month moratorium on the conversion of residential housing units into commercial office space. They intend to bring furniture and paint to the City Council chamber.

The planned action panics a councilman who backs the moratorium idea. "That is an incredibly stupid thing to say and threaten," sputters Alan Taylor. "I trust the police officials won't allow any of that in the door." HART activists move in anyway, bringing lamps, rugs, tables and signs that demand an end to housing conversions.

Ultimately, spurred on by a citywide housing movement, the Council passes an historic "Housing Preservation and Restoration" law, which requires developers to replace or fund housing they eliminate when they build new office buildings.

The Trucks Stop Here
June 23, 1986

On this summer day, two dozen residents step out into the middle of Stone Street in Hartford's south end. They create a human wall that stops all the big trucks in their path.

These 75,000 lb. monsters shake the foundations of the buildings they pass; the din of noisy brakes and diesel engines is unrelenting. "This is democracy at work, civil disobedience, without harm to anyone," says neighborhood leader Flora Long on June 23, 1986. "The people of this neighborhood have no other way to show the city how we feel."

Stone Street is in a quiet neighborhood, home to elderly residents and families with children. But as many as ninety-eight construction trucks *an hour* rumble past their homes, shaking the foundations. Stone, Burlington and Dart Streets are the route

Area Residents Halt Trucks

Stone Street residents block traffic, 1986 (Homefront archives)

that the big rigs use-- especially those from the Balf Company, a local sand and gravel supplier -- to reach the highway six days a week.

Back in 1975, resident Mary Maloney engaged Neighborhood Legal Services lawyer Pamela Hershinson to win a state regulation banning the heavy volume of truck traffic. The decision was later overturned by a legislative committee, so Mary successfully sued the state. In 1980 Hartford city officials set up an asphalt barrier to stop all traffic. The ban was appealed by Balf to the state Supreme Court. The company also sued the city for $6 million.

Now the Stone Street neighbors fear the worst: a "compromise" between the city council and Balf that will permanently allow the heavy trucks to roll and get Hartford out from under the lawsuit.

Three weeks after the first street action, the residents once again use their bodies to block the trucks, this time with 100 people. They allow cars to pass.

The current truck route through Stone Street takes two minutes to reach the highway, they explain. If the trucks use a different route it takes six minutes. It's a case of profit over people.

The blockades are mounted two more times in July, ending only when the police force the protesters to leave. Stone Street becomes a nonviolent battlefield. Some of the truck drivers are angry at the delays; others support the neighborhood activists.

On August 13, a 76 year-old man crossing a nearby street is struck by a Balf truck. The residents block traffic once again, this time with a mock coffin. The pedestrian dies a few days later.

The fight ends when Balf agrees to cut its truck traffic up to fifty per cent, lower their speed, and end all weekend traffic. It also withdraws its lawsuit. Residents say they are not fully satisfied. But a struggle that had gone on for ten years without a solution ends in three months after they mount their direct action, stepping off their sidewalks and into the street.

Linkage Blockade
June 24, 1986

Angry at the Hartford City Council's refusal to support a major community effort to increase jobs and housing, forty neighborhood activists block the Interstate 84 exit near Aetna Insurance at the morning rush hour. "No More Business as Usual" proclaim the flyers they distribute to commuters. Aetna denies any responsibility for killing the bill. "We stand on our record of social responsibility," says a corporate spokesman.

The night before the traffic blockade, Council members voted 7 to 1 against the Linkage ordinance which would require private developers to pay a fee on new commercial office space. The fee would be used to rehabilitate housing and create job training. The community activists demonstrate that the city loses jobs and housing every time a new corporation moves into town, bringing outside employees with them, which further limits affordable housing.

Aetna is the insurance giant that has quietly scuttled the year-long Linkage negotiations between city officials and neighborhood groups. A secret memo from Aetna's CEO, chastising city officials and other corporate leaders for making any agreement, is exposed just before the two sides are ready to reach a compromise that could pass at City Council.

Not surprisingly, the blockade has its critics. "I just think from my involvement in civil rights, they are not going to get much support from those activities," sniffs Norvel Goff, the City Council's majority leader. Goff had run on a pro-Linkage platform to get elected. He has voted against the ordinance.

The anger of those who worked on the failed linkage campaign does not end with the blockade. They pledge to build a third political party in Hartford. In the next City Council election, "People For Change" successfully challenges the incumbent Council members who have reneged on their promises.

Protest Camp at the Library:
Mark Twain Would Approve
July, 2008

The first time they tried to close branch libraries was in June, 1932. The Hartford Public Library (HPL) financial committee targeted three branches "with the smallest circulation:" Blue Hills, Southwest and the Mark Twain branch. Together, 213,051 books were checked out annually at these three locations.

Ultimately the local libraries were saved, although through the years, financial pressures kept them in danger of returning to the chopping block. In the summer of 1977, all Hartford Public libraries were closed for the season, even the main branch, to save money.

Now, in 2008 the library bosses announce that the Mark Twain's last day will be Friday, July 4th. The local block club plans a "read-in" to protest the closing of this community resource. "When we fill all the seats in the library we will sit on the grass outside," says one of the neighbors.

Nineteen workers will lose their jobs. Management is using the job loss threat to press for employee concessions. Library board president Geraldine Sullivan says the branch is losing money. She says nothing about the Hartford Library system's $14 million unrestricted endowment.

Sam Clemens
(Napoleon Sarony photo, 1895)

As the story reaches more people, a protest camp grows on the small lawn in front of the Farmington Avenue branch. Signs and banners appear and people visit at all hours.

City-wide organizing saves the two branches, and by September, the city and the state have bailed the library out with $250,000. The city also says it will audit the HPL books.

Mark Twain struggles along, neglected by the HPL administration. The branch is forced to close half the time in the summer of 2010 due to faulty electrical wiring, says union Vice President and Mark Twain employee Dave Ionno.

Finally, on June 21, 2011, the Board of Education approves moving the Mark Twain branch to Hartford High School. The school has a library with very few books, so it's a good fit, if not an ideal location for the public.

The new site is just a block from Samuel Clemens' historic home on Forest Street. Before the house was restored, it served as a library branch.

Work/Labor

"We Irish Are a Working Race."
March 3, 1849

The angry Irish laborers march from Hartford to East Hartford across the old covered bridge that spans the Connecticut River. They converge at the home of their boss. As a contractor, he hired the immigrants to help build the Hartford/Providence railroad.

The Irish had done their work and they expected to be paid. But without warning, the contractor declared he was bankrupt and closed his business without compensating the men he hired.

When the workers arrive at the contractor's home they demand their back pay. The boss has nothing to say. He will wait them out, sure that the police will come soon. They don't.

The workers surround the house. If the boss won't come out to them, he won't be allowed to leave at all. Finally, after three days, the police escort the contractor from his home. History does not record the end result of this siege. Take into account, however, that it takes *three days* for the authorities to arrive. They were clearly in no hurry to interfere with the laborers' cause.

When the sheriff finally shows up, he removes the boss without a fight from the men at the blockade. Most certainly, a deal has been struck for the workers' wages.

Irish laborers, 1860s
(Yesteryear's News)

These immigrants have fled from *An Gorta Mor*, the Great Hunger in Ireland of the 1840's. The "famine" began with the potato crop failure, but English laws and wealthy Irish landlords extract millions of pounds of food for profit, instead of feeding starving Irish families.

The Hartford laborers have lived this horror once already, and won't be cheated again.

Factory Girls Strike for Their Health
March 18, 1907

The factory owner implements a sixty-hour work week from the young women employed at the Government Envelope Works on South Ann Street. But apparently this is still not enough for the boss, so he orders "his girls" to work into the night on a regular basis.

Piecework rates for a six-day week earn the female employees between $5 and $9. At the same time, the average union construction worker earns at least $18 a week for about 49 hours work.

The young women are tired of working in excess of 80 hours a week, and some of them decide to act. One woman, and then seven more night workers

Young factory workers, circa 1910 (Yesteryear's News)

refuse the mandatory overtime. Actually, they have only refused to work more than two additional nights a week, but the boss considers this insubordination. They are fired.

The envelope factory is doing well. It has established an evening shift in order to keep up with demand. The first shift begins at 7:00 a.m. and ends at 5:00 p.m. Any department that is short means the earlier shift is forced to stay on the job. Any girl who is even a minute late for work will be locked out for that day.

The young women declare that the 80 hours or more spent at their machines is dangerous to their health. Advocates like the Consumers League of Connecticut agree.

The League has been created to address sweatshop conditions. For the 4,000 factories operating in the state in 1907, the state government has only three factory inspectors. At a conference at the Center Church in Hartford, Professor Willard C. Fisher calls factory inspection "little better than a farce." The Government Envelope factory workers already know that.

When the eight women are fired, the overtime situation only gets worse. On March 18th, fifty factory workers walk out to protest the intolerable conditions. Now production comes to a dead stop.

Within a day, the eight are back to work. An "amicable agreement" is made to end the forced overtime.

"Something to Show for Our Work:"
The Unemployed Organize
August 1933

Brainard Field may well be the country's first municipal airport. Located in a former cow pasture in southeast Hartford, Brainard opens in 1921. The era's greatest aviators– Amelia Earhart and Charles Lindbergh– land there to great acclaim. For its first decade, the field is used primarily for passenger flights.

Brainard Airfield, circa 1920
(Hartford History Center)

But in 1933, as the Great Depression tightens its grip, city officials decide Brainard should accommodate commercial traffic to spur the economy. This will require expansion and turning the grass airstrip runways into blacktop pavement. How can the work be done on the cheap? With the city's ever-growing number of jobless workers, of course. City employees who drove ash wagons have already been replaced by jobless men- a great savings to the city.

In August, 1933 the city's public welfare department advertises for the Brainard project. One hundred workers are hired. Most are family men, now desperate for jobs. They had worked in local factories as machinists, assemblers, laborers and office clerks before massive layoffs occurred.

The unemployed men have heard they are to be paid 40 cents an hour. Unfortunately for them, there are no wages, only food subsidies and partial rent payments. Work starts at 7:30 am. Most of the men have to walk three or more miles to reach the airfield. They are told that if they don't have sufficient food to eat for lunch they should try to get a private charity to assist them.

Married men without children are restricted to working a maximum of 2 1/2 days a week. Men with four or more children are allowed to work 5 1/2 days a week.

Relief as Punishment

The jobs are "compulsory," announces Hartford welfare superintendent William J. Ryan. If any of the men are hired but then refuse to work, and later apply for public assistance, they will be arrested for nonsupport. The Brainard job will give the men "the opportunity to regain their self -respect," Ryan declares, with no apparent irony.

The men have a different view. "I can't work for nothing," complains one. "I have to make payments on furniture." Others speak of insurance premiums to meet, doctor bills to pay, kids' clothing to buy. "Now all we need are a ball and chain," observes one man. "Conditions like that are enough to turn anyone into a radical," another worker says.

Federal relief programs are still several years away. Most welfare, as meager as it is, comes from local sources. The popular theory is to make public assistance as difficult as possible to obtain, in order to discourage dependence. Welfare violates the American spirit of pride and self-sufficiency, according to policy makers.

Outright refusal to provide government support isn't necessary, the noted sociologist Frances Fox Piven has written. If receiving aid is made degrading enough, recipients become outcasts. Early in the dispute, Hartford Mayor Walter Batterson warns that if the men are paid wages, they will buy alcohol instead of providing for their families.

The Men Fight Back

The day after the project begins, as word spreads there will be no wages at all, dozens of men throw down their picks and shovels. A strike is on. The action is led by former railroad man Martin Meaney and by Will Thomas, an African American mechanic. They are supported by a multiracial committee and quickly meet with Mayor Batterson.

"We like to feel that no matter how small the wages, we have something to show for our work," one committeeman tells him.   The dispute is settled when the mayor guarantees that no one will be arrested for refusing the outdoor work. The men agree to $1.00 a day plus their food and rent assistance. Two buses from Main and Gold Streets will transport them to and from the job site each day.

The Gandhi Strike
April 10, 1935

Hartford's first sit-down strike takes place at the Capewell Horseshoe Nail Company on Charter Oak Avenue in the Dutch Point neighborhood. It begins on April 10,1935. In its day, Capewell has produced two-thirds of all the horseshoe nails bought in the U.S., and employs over one thousand workers. But by the 1930s, automobiles (like the Chevrolets made in Flint, Michigan) have replaced horse travel and Capewell's employees now total no more than one hundred.

The Capewell factory is organized into three different collective bargaining units. The Machinists Union and the Horse Nail Makers are male-dominated. The Assorters and Packers Union is made up exclusively of women. All three have a history of fighting and winning strikes in 1902, and 1916, and a successful fight for the eight-hour day in 1913.

Now in 1935 Capewell workers petition the state

labor department after the employer refuses to bargain with them. This legal strategy produces little success. In April, Capewell lays off eight workers. The boss says that business is slow, which is probably true. But the workers identify another motive behind the layoffs: union busting. Five of the eight are union men, including the chair of the shop committee.

When the union demands reinstatement of the men and is rebuffed, the workers sit "with folded arms in front of their benches," one newspaper reports. The tactic is also called a "Gandhi strike" in the press, referring to the extraordinary Indian leader who is fighting British colonialism, using effective acts of nonviolent noncooperation. The Mahatma has already led South African miners and Indian textile workers in powerful strikes.

Two days later the Capewell workforce walks out of the factory, shutting down production. Within a month the union reaches agreement for a fair distribution of available work, bringing back those who have been laid off.

The Colt 45: Peace Work with a Union Label
May 13, 1986

The Colt Firearms factory has been producing guns since the 1800s, from pistols to Gatling guns and now, M-16 automatic weapons. The Colt name is known worldwide. Workers at Colt have tried to establish a union since the turn of the 20th century, and finally succeed in the 1940s.

Supporters block factory entrance. Teachers' Union president George Springer, center (Nick Lacy)

Now, in 1986, they are in a life or death struggle with a company that will do anything to break their union, United Auto Workers (UAW) Local 376. Colt intends to rollback the gains made over the years by the white, black, and Puerto Rican workforce. "We are not claiming that we are losing money, nor were we basing our proposals on the Company's financial condition," admits the company's top negotiator.

Colt workers have already been protesting on the inside for more than a year against poor treatment and blatant attempts to bust their union. Led by shop chairman Lester Harding, activists have been disciplined, suspended and fired for nonexistent infractions. In response, they print the names of the fired workers on their shirts, and parade in the plant during break time to communicate their anger.

Once the strike begins on January 24 1986, the 1,000 strikers attempt to stop scabs from entering the factory and taking their jobs. Frequent scuffles on the picket line are met with overwhelming force by the city police. There are many arrests during the strike's first months. At one point UAW leader Phil Wheeler is slapped with inciting a riot, a serious felony charge.

The boss at Colt knows that public opinion is important in this fight. He thinks he can sway that opinion with full-page newspaper ads. He harps on the picket line conflicts, laying the blame solely on the strikers. He explains how reasonable his negotiating demands are, and how unreasonable the UAW is.

Thanks to the newly formed Labor/Community Alliance, the propaganda falls flat. On May 13 1986, forty-five community activists, elected officials, clergy members, teachers and others converge on the Colt factory on Huyshope Avenue, Hartford. They sit down, blocking the parking lot entrance and the scabs attempting to enter the factory. The group is dubbed the "Colt 45," an ironic take on the company's most famous product.

The civil disobedience is no picnic. The Hartford Police captain in charge of the cops on the line has be accused of acting against the strikers from the beginning. The workers are proven correct when he quits the police force during the strike and takes a job as the new head of security for Colt.

The nonviolent Colt 45 action is only one of many community support events and marches organized during the record four-year struggle. Critical to the strikers' morale is the solidarity they get from other unions and the city and state lawmakers, who support a successful nationwide boycott of Colt products. In fact, the strike itself is the longest sustained nonviolent action in Connecticut history.

Included in the Colt 45 are a number of peace activists. Is this some mistake? No, they say. They issue a public statement signed by many of the most locally prominent anti-war figures, who explain that union jobs are good for families and neighborhoods. They understand that workers have no power to choose what they make in this society.

The activists want to build relationships with unions and rank-and-file workers to find common ground and ultimately achieve "economic conversion," the process by which industry changes to peacetime production. There are only two sides in this fight, and they choose the workers.

In 1990, UAW 376 wins big. The company finally gives in after labor court decisions have found that Colt has been a massive law breaker. Workers win $10 million in back pay and benefits. All strikers can return to their jobs. A coalition of the state government, private investors-- and the UAW-- have bought the company.

Thirty years later, union veterans and community activists hold a "commemoration of courage" to celebrate the Colt strikers' victory. At first, some openly question the event's purpose: do they really want to remember those hard times? But still, many strikers and their spouses attend. When asked about good memories from their historic strike, they answer "the Colt 45."

"They Treat the Worker Badly": Striking for Respect
August, 1986

The union organizer walks into the office of Joseph Ramondetta, owner of Futuramik, Inc. He brings a priest and a newspaper reporter with him. The organizer hands the owner a first aid kit. The workers at this Hartford factory have burns on their arms from the molten plastic used to form appliance parts. The work is hazardous and dirty; at least their injuries should be treated.

Ramondetta refuses the organizer's offer. The Puerto Rican workers will just steal the first aid box, the boss says.

Danny Perez (standing, second from left) with ILGWU workers (Thornton)

The organizer is Danny Perez, who has been sent

from the International Ladies Garment Workers Union (ILGWU) in New York to help these workers protect their union. The owner has been stonewalling and won't bargain in good faith. But now, Ramondetta's latest insult is the spark Perez needs to mobilize the Futuramik employees.

The reporter who has witnessed the owner's racist reaction publishes a story about it in his newspaper column. Perez takes the morning edition to the factory. The workers stop their machines as he reads the news article to them.

Fed up with the boss's disrespect, almost 200 workers walk off the job. One worker sums it all up: *"Tratan mal al obrero,"* they treat the worker badly. The strike is on.

These low-wage workers should not have had to strike in order to achieve union benefits. The workforce voted to unionize in 1977. Neglect by the regional union office (and, no doubt, manipulation by the boss) resulted in the workers rejecting union representation a few years later.

In 1984, however, the workers once again take a union vote. The boss wins, but only by flagrant violations of labor laws. A federal agency orders a new election. On May 30, 1986, the workers vote again and win. Ramondetta stalls with legal maneuvers.

Ten days after the "first aid kit strike" starts, the boss gives in and respects the workers' choice. They now have their union. ILGWU conducts a survey to see what workplace safety features are needed, and the boss begins to make improvements.

"I like the little guy beating up the big guy," Danny Perez says.

Huelga de Brazos Caido: Justice for Janitors
September 26, 2000

Unionized janitors and student activists of the Connecticut Global Action Network (CGAN) come together to make the connections between global corporate greed and the fight for a living wage. Twenty-five people are arrested for blocking downtown traffic at rush hour in front of United Technologies' (UTC) "Gold Building."

Designed to coincide with international days of action against the World Bank and IMF, the protest has focused on SEIU Local 531's (now SEIU 32-BJ) current fight on behalf of hundreds of janitors who clean office buildings in Hartford and the surrounding suburbs.

Cleaners in the burbs do the same work and are employed by the same contractors as city janitors, but are paid less and don't have health insurance.

UTC is targeted because the giant producer of aircraft engines recently fired its unionized janitorial workforce and replaced the crew with lower paid, non-union workers. United Technologies has also been accused by the Machinists' Union of shipping jobs overseas in violation of their collective bargaining agreement.

The action is a prelude to the strike deadline that Local 531 has set if the demands for decent wages and benefits are not met.

Two weeks after the traffic blockade, the Union settles with cleaning contractors for more full-time jobs in the suburbs and pay raises for city and suburban janitors.

Locked Out, Not Knocked Down
February 27, 2003

"I'm 82 years old and if I get arrested they'll get the message," says Charlotte Kaminski of Newington, a former Machinists' union steward at the Emhart company. Charlotte's daughter is a nurse and a laid-off state employee.

Over 2,000 people march and chant in opposition to Governor John G. Rowland's budget deficit plan, which they say will destroy state services for disabled and poor people. The demonstrators include unionized state employees, community groups, human service advocates and college students whose programs are being shut down.

Police arrest more than 50 demonstrators who block the main entrance to the State Capitol during the protest just after Rowland's "slash and burn" budget is approved by the legislature. Three thousand state employees are being laid off as a result of the cuts.

Rowland's staff is told to stay home in anticipation of the protest. "Several thousand people indicated in advance they intended to break the law," Rowland spokesman Chris Cooper says. "In this particular time we live in, you can't be too careful."

The demonstrators issue a statement which they entitle "No Business as Usual." It reads, in part:

"We are here today because the governor and legislative leaders have locked out 3000 state workers from their jobs-- people who protect the public health, ensure public safety, and provide dignity for our most vulnerable citizens.

"In response, we are locking out the Governor and Legislative leadership from the State Capitol.

"During this nonviolent direct action, we are holding photographs of some of the people who are the real targets of John Rowland's layoffs and budget cuts. We are here because they cannot be here.

"We risk arrest because of them... the pain caused by John Rowland and legislative leaders is real. This action is part of our continuing pledge to win a Fair Share budget for these people and all the people of our state."

The crowd cheers for Charlotte Kaminski as she is taken away by the police.

Moral Monday Turn Up
April 4, 2016

The Hartford City Council is ready to vote. On tonight's agenda is the private takeover of the city employee workforce. Only three months into his job, Mayor Luke Bronin is planning to end the budget deficit, in part by lowering wages and benefits for hundreds of working men and women.

Bronin's scheme is not a new one: select an "oversight board" with a majority of unelected business leaders to make decisions that have for years been subject to union collective bargaining. It was done in Bridgeport, Warebury, and other cities, so why not Hartford? Bronin is ambitious and union bashing looks good on the resume.

Bishop John Selders on a union picket line (Thornton)

Union members have been alerted, and they plan to speak out against what Councilwoman Wildaliz Bermudez calls a "authoritarian power grab." In recent times the unions have been rarely able to halt municipal bosses from shaving away their benefits and have lost many jobs to outside bidding, where wages are lower and workers have no due process protections. Still, they are always first to be called to sacrifice.

Tonight, AFSCME Local 1716 and other union members almost fill the council hearing chamber. They receive an unexpected boost from Moral Monday CT, a grassroots social justice group led by Bishop John and Pamela Selders. It's patterned after the successful nonviolent direct action movement created by Rev. William Barber in North Carolina.

Selders and cohorts flood the large room; they are not about to be quiet and wait their turn to speak. "Ninety days and a power grab!" they chant as Bronin walks into to chamber. In the midst of noise, confusion, and critical mass of city people, union supporters and angry opponents of the business coup speak their minds.

Bronin's proposal goes down in flames by a vote of 8-1. Several council people later admit that they voted "no" after witnessing the groundswell of public opposition.

Bishop Selders calls the direct action practice *Turn Up*, to "generate a crisis, which creates the political space for community change and transformation."

Civil Rights

Breaking the UPS Race Barrier
May 14, 1965

One by one the young Black and white protestors approach the United Parcel Service (UPS) parking lot on Locust Street. It is May 14, 1965. In unison, they sit down at the lot's entrance, blocking the mammoth trucks that are delivering packages to the city and beyond. The police are waiting. Ten activists, including Henry Hurvitz, are arrested; some refuse to leave and are carried to the police wagon.

The patience of local civil rights organizers has been sorely tested. Since 1963, Wilber Smith, president of the Hartford NAACP, had been urging UPS to end its discriminatory hiring practices. At the time the company had only one African American worker, employed as a car washer. When activists threatened to demonstrate in front of the UPS facility, four more black workers were hired. UPS is blaming white suburban housewives who will "object" to having their packages brought to them by black men.

Progress is much too slow, until NECAP enters

the scene. The North End Community Action Program, founded in 1963, is an offshoot of the Northern Student Movement. The Hartford group focuses on race discrimination in housing and jobs. They take on slumlords with tenant rent strikes; several landlords capitulate and improve their buildings. They picket restaurants such as Carville's and Terry Square Diner with some success. Travelers Insurance, the Statler Hilton hotel and Korvettes department store are targets of the group's pickets as well.

In solidarity with the Student Nonviolent Coordinating Committee (SNCC), NECAP and UCONN students mount a picket in December, 1963 at the Toddle House, part of a national restaurant chain. Twenty-one SNCC members had just been arrested at the Toddle House franchise in Atlanta, Georgia after being refused service (two Connecticut activists were among those arrested), and the Hartford activists march to show their support.

Now, after fruitless efforts to commit UPS to fair hiring practices, the NECAP youths put their bodies on the line. One day after the Georgia arrests, the group announces its plan to escalate their campaign by picketing the Hartford Chamber of Commerce. On May 19th, three NECAP members occupy the Chamber's office on Constitution Plaza and are arrested for trespassing. At this point NECAP has the attention of City Hall and Governor John Dempsey. Elected officials scramble to sit down with the UPS regional bosses to see how the dispute can be resolved.

Within two weeks, UPS officials publicly pledge to hire eight African Americans– at all job levels– and create a special recruiting program for "minority and disadvantaged people." The company also drops the charges against the "NECAP 10." The student group moves on to its next target.

Turn Left or Be Shot
August 17, 1965

This summer, cities have been burning: Watts, Chicago, New York. Despair has turned to rage in Black and Latino communities, fueled by racism, chronic poverty, second-rate education and substandard health care.

The North End Community Action Project (NECAP) organizes to fill the void between social service agencies and Hartford's decision makers.

On a hot August night, 300 people rally in a north end parking lot. Protesters march down Main Street to City Hall with a symbolic black coffin representing the deaths of their friends and neighbors at the hands of the police.

"Turn left or be shot" reads one of their homemade signs, a direct reference to the recent National Guard warning to protesters in the Watts neighborhood of Los Angeles. At least 23 black people have been killed in Watts, mostly by the police.

It's 10:00 pm, and City Hall is closed. Forty of the marchers sit at the front door steps. Sixty cops are bused in to disperse them. There has been no indication of violent behavior on the part of the crowd.

The event is specifically designed to emphasize the fact that civil rights marches like these are being met with police violence. "Their theme was that Negroes long have been victims of oppression by whites," reports a local newspaper. As if to prove their point, the police arrest nine of the protesters.

Poverty and Power Collide
September 14, 1966

The judge says he respects the ideals of Fred Harris from the Hill Parents Association, but then chides the activist for using the wrong tactics. Harris receives 90 days in jail.

In 1965, a total of 16 people had entered the State welfare commissioner's Asylum Street office as part of a larger demonstration supported by CORE and SNCC. Now, more than a year later, those arrested are on trial. The defendants include Hartford's Wilber Smith and John Wilhelm, a recent Yale graduate. The group seeks to shine a light on the inadequacy of the state's efforts to provide services to the poor.

Also in the group are three state employees, welfare caseworkers who sympathize with the protest. "We were there in sympathy with the people on welfare who marched," says Marianne Carlet.

The protest launches at least a few of the protesters into a lifelong quest for social justice. Wilber Smith becomes a civil rights leader and eventually a State Senator. John Wilhelm joins the labor movement and leads the 230,000 members of UNITE HERE.

Fred Harris ends up serving a 30-day sentence at Hartford's notorious Seyms Street jail, located in the city's poorest neighborhood. While imprisoned, he is appointed to an advisory committee for New Haven's community college.

Just before dawn on the morning of his release, Harris is given a hero's welcome by 100 supporters who take him home in a 25-car caravan.

The People's Legislature
April 22, 1969

Three hundred angry Hartford residents stream into the State Capitol, climbing to the Hall of the House on the second floor. The hall is the largest chamber in the building. Many of the protesters jam the gallery while others occupy the seats of state legislators who are taking a break.

The group demands a meeting with the Appropriations Committee. "Where are the dudes with the money?" yells one young man into a lawmaker's microphone. His amplified voice stops all conversations. "We're not going anywhere until the dudes show up!"

Activists Isabel Blake and Ned Coll are on the

500 Invade State Capitol In Welfare Cuts Protest

Agency Role On Vaccine Under Fire

By ROBERT WATERS
Washington Correspondent

WASHINGTON — A little-known federal agency that is supposed to supervise the manufacture, test and sale of vaccines will come under sharp attack in the Senate today in documents to be released by Sen. Abraham A. Ribicoff, D-Conn.

The agency is the Division of Biologics Standards (DBS)—an arm of the Department of Health, Education and Welfare (HEW).

Ribicoff, in remarks prepared for the Senate, will charge that DBS claims it has "no responsibility to test vaccines for effectiveness."

The documents to be cited by Ribicoff were made available to the Connecticut Democrat's subcommittee on executive reorganization by Dr. J. Anthony Morris, a DBS research microbiologist, and James Turner, a former associate of consumer advocate Ralph Nader. Turner is conducting independent consumer research and is the author of a book called "The Chemical Feast."

'Dubious Techniques'

Their information, according to the Ribicoff subcommittee, alleges that DBS relied on "dubious techniques" for testing an influenza vaccine in use today; tampered with the results of the tests; and discouraged scientific research which might have cast doubt on the agency.

They also allege that DBS ignored scientific data indicating that a cold vaccine widely used in the early '60s contained material which could cause cancer.

Another claim cited in the documents Ribicoff will make public is that DBS disregarded evidence that could have prevented the use of contaminated polio vaccine which led to the paralysis of 150 persons in 1955.

In his formal remarks in the Senate today, Ribicoff will call on HEW Secretary Elliot L. Richardson to investigate the

Calm Before ...

An unidentified welfare demonstrator prays in the hall of the State House of Representatives Thursday morning shortly after a group of about 500 demonstrators took over

the hall. They were protesting cuts in welfare payments and the announced policy of block payments to recipients (Courant Photo by Harry Batz).

Legislator Bloodied In Melee

By KENNETH HOOKER

A legislator was slightly injured Thursday during an invasion of the state capitol by a group of angry downstate demonstrators protesting cuts and block payments to welfare recipients.

Rep. Charles C. Grah, R-Canterbury, suffered cuts on his face when he was beaten while trying to protect Rep. Astrid T. Hanzalek, R-Suffield, in a melee in the capitol halls. Sen. David O. Odegard, R-Manchester, also was involved.

The fight was the only outright violence during day-long disruptions by about 500 demonstrators who had hoped to see Gov. Meskill or Welfare Commissioner Henry C. White.

About 40 of the demonstrators camped out on the capitol lawn Thursday night and promised to continue the demonstration until their demands are met.

The group began by camping in front of the governor's office and later took over the chamber of the State House of Representatives, where they said they would wait until either the governor or White addressed them. Unavailable

Neither official appeared, nor was either available for comment. The governor had left the office about 10 minutes before the first of about a dozen buses carrying the demonstrators arrived.

The violence erupted after a group of about 75 demonstrators broke up a meeting of the General Assembly's Education Committee on the fourth floor of the building about 3 p.m.

"There will be no meeting in this building until there is a welfare meeting," a young man told the assembled legislators conducting a hearing on state aid to private schools.

After about 25 minutes of shouting between the demonstrators and Rep. Howard M. Klebanoff and Sen. Wilber G. Smith, both Hartford Demo-

News media hype often exaggerated nonviolent protests at the State Capitol, as with this 1971 protest. (Homefront archives)

House floor, both veterans of social justice fights, side by side with younger militants from Hartford's streets. Joining them are local clergy and area college students who have been volunteering to work with disadvantaged youth.

They have one purpose: restoring the 40% cut in aid to the poor, caused by the state and federal social funds that are being diverted to the war in Vietnam. Some of the protesters begin quiet dialogues with the few legislators who, unlike their colleagues, have not left the hall for the safety of their offices.

"We don't have anything to say to you," a Bridgeport Democrat tells the occupiers. But this "people's legislature" refuses to move until they are finally guaranteed a meeting with the Appropriations chairman.

Puerto Rican Youths Create a "Liberated Space"
November 23, 1970

Just after dark, a dozen young Puerto Ricans approach 21 Kennedy Street, an abandoned building near Keney Tower. Within minutes they are inside, establishing the space as a liberated area to be used for a breakfast program, free clothing distribution and drop-in center. Hartford Police show up but take no action against the teenagers, who call themselves the Peoples Liberation Party (PLP).

The day of the occupation, November 23, 1970,

Naming the people's center (Homefront archives)

coincides with a surge in community anger over police brutality. Abraham Rodriguez, an unarmed nineteen-year old, had been killed the previous spring by Officer Anthony Lombardi (subsequently fired by the police department). A recent small disturbance at the Lyric Dance Hall on Park Street turned into a police riot where women and men were indiscriminately beaten.

The PLP is influenced by the Young Lords Party, a New York City group that has been engaging in militant community organizing. The Lords have occupied an empty church and use it as a community center. They commandeer an unused medical testing truck to conduct the TB tests that would otherwise not be available.

And in their boldest move, the Young Lords take over Lincoln Hospital in the South Bronx on July 14th in protest of the substandard care the city provides. In solidarity, most of the hospital staff stay in the facility as well and continue their work.

As described by 17 year-old Jose Claudio, the PLP's leader, the Kennedy Street building, owned by the Hartford Housing Authority, is one of many abandoned buildings throughout the city's north end. Now the structure will have a purpose, he says, as party members paint the walls and fix the water pipes.

In less than a month, the group has set up a second site at the South Park Methodist Church. They plan to provide political education classes and work on the desperate living conditions in their neighborhoods. The community space is called the Abraham Rodriguez Memorial Center.

Isabel Blake, Welfare Warrior
October 13, 1971

Isabel Blake challenges state legislators to "meet with us and talk things over." The legislators stay silent. "We don't bite," Blake says. "We don't have much to eat, but we don't eat people."

Isabel Blake has raised ten children in Hartford. She is recognized as a top leader of the local poor people's movement, advocating for public housing residents and welfare recipients. By 1971, she heads up Welfare Mothers' Rights and plays an active role in the statewide group Welfare Recipients Are People (WRAP).

The group's target is Governor Thomas Meskill, a Nixon-like conservative who calls the state's welfare system "a monster" and proceeds to cut assistance to recipients. In just one day he vetoes tax breaks for low- and moderate-income housing, funding for vocational training in the prisons (just two months before New York's Attica prison rebellion), and a procedure that would make it easier for welfare recipients to save for a rent deposit.

Worst of all, the legislature has established the "flat grant " payment system that will mean cuts to rental assistance. "Flat grants are lower rent standards in disguise," says Blake. The activists draw up a list of written

Isabel Blake, welfare warrior (Hartford History Center)

demands ending with "Stop playing God. You're no better than we are and we are all human beings."

Blake and other leaders plan an October 13th rally at Bushnell Park, which borders the State Capitol. The event coincides with a demonstration against the Vietnam war. Locally, peace activists are making the connections between the war's rising costs and the resulting cuts in domestic programs: $40 billion (in today's dollars) has been cut in recent years. "You want us to work but you won't train us, provide us with day care or help us get jobs. You deceive poor people," Blake angrily declares.

The protest is now the state's big news. Taking advantage of the spotlight, the protesters personally deliver their rent payments to Henry White, Meskill's welfare commissioner. The cutbacks planned for November 1st will make it even tougher to pay the rent. White refuses the money but the activists have made their point.

The welfare moms, backed by churches and progressive groups, spend October 13th inside the State Capitol to lobby legislators. "Violence in State Capitol" reads a panicky newspaper headline. "The violence is being done to families by totally unjust cuts in family budgets," says a spokesperson for the local Basic Human Rights Coalition.

Daily lobbying and rallies soon develop into a tent city on the Capitol lawn. More than 100 people stay overnight and others join by day. Meskill publicly threatens to break up the protest by force. "Are you ready to go to jail?" reporters ask Blake. "I'm ready to go to hell" she replies.

Just before dawn on October 20th, Hartford police raid the camp and arrest Blake and Francesca Cruz, a Puerto Rican community leader who alerts the other occupiers by loudspeaker before she can be stopped.

Support grows for the tent city and their demands. The state chapter of Vietnam Veterans Against the War (VVAW) occupies the Capitol grounds overnight in solidarity with the two welfare protest leaders. Nine-year old Aida Rivera delivers a devils food cake to the Governor's office with the words "Meskill the Blue-Eyed Devil" neatly printed in frosting.

On the tent city's sixteenth day, a judge grants an injunction against the November cuts. It's a temporary win in a longer fight, but as community leader Ramon Quiros tells the occupiers at their victory party, "this is a night of celebration."

The jury trial of Blake and Cruz finally takes place a year after the arrests. They are both acquitted. "Will you go back to the Capitol?" she is asked. "No. Just wait and see what I do," Isabel Blake replies.

Anti-War

Anti-War Vets Take the Armory, Occupy a Church
December 30, 1971

Nothing strange about military veterans walking into the State Armory on Capitol Avenue. The nine men head for the office of Connecticut's top National Guard commander.

That's when onlookers realize these aren't just *any* veterans; they are members of Vietnam Veterans Against the War (VVAW). Their purpose is not to visit Major General E. Donald Walsh, but to occupy his office in protest of the ongoing war in Southeast Asia.

Led by Jack Smith, the vets remove a military flag hanging in Walsh's office. They replace it with their own Connecticut VVAW flag. Then they wait. Soon enough, about a dozen state police arrive and order them to leave. The protesters refuse, and one by one they are arrested and placed in the police wagon.

VVAW direct action plays a crucial role in the movement against the Vietnam war. Their shocking first-hand testimony at the national "Winter Soldier" hearings in Washington D.C., exposing how the war is really being waged, puts the lie to government propaganda. The vets themselves confess to atrocities they and other soldiers have been committing against the Vietnamese people.

In Hartford and around the state, these ex-soldiers can be found at every anti-war demonstration, on college campuses, and sometimes in unexpected places. At Easter time, 1972, VVAW invades St. Joseph's Cathedral on Farmington Avenue. Dressed in their military uniforms, they carry a black coffin into the enormous church. Silently they maintain their presence throughout the service. No one dares to make a scene by calling the police.

Painted on the side of the coffin are the words "300 won't rise today," referring to the daily number of Vietnamese casualties. "This is the day when Christ is supposed to have risen," says Jake Jacobson, a former Green Beret. "But 300 Vietnamese people won't rise."

He and the other VVAW members also have another message for the church. They are insisting that religious groups disclose how they invest their money so the public can find out where the Church owns stock in weapon companies. "It's hypocritical that people should come here to pray for peace when the church owns securities in war-producing companies," Jacobson says.

Mining the Connecticut River
May 10, 1972

Mysterious metal drums float down the Connecticut

River. The Hartford Police call out their bomb squad. Good thing, too. The drums have "Blam!" painted on their sides.

Richard Nixon's Vietnam War has escalated. Now he has decided to mine the North Vietnamese harbors and bomb roads and rail networks, a devastating attack on the civilian infrastructure.

Anti-war protesters have called the press early on May 10, 1972 to announce that they have "mined" the river. "The mines in Haiphong Harbor are real. Ours are not," says a young woman who only identifies herself as 'Anita of Earth.' "Ours cannot kick off a world war. Do what is necessary to make yourself heard."

That same day, 30 University of Hartford students block the driveway of the Governor's mansion on Prospect Street. "Governor Meskill supports Nixon's escalation of the war," they declare.

Women Beat Oppressive Grand Jury
December 20, 1975

In 1970, American students shut down hundreds of schools and universities across the nation after the illegal U.S. bombing of Cambodia and the killings of four young people at Kent State in Ohio and two in Jackson State, Mississippi. The year marks a new decade of war in Vietnam, the FBI targeting of civil rights leaders, and a president who calls students bums and draws up an "enemies list." It also marks a new phase for lesbian and gay liberation.

This year, some won't wait for a mass movement to stop the violence and imperial excesses of the United States. Hartford native Susan Saxe, Katherine Power and a handful of others rob a Massachusetts bank in 1970 "for the revolution" and a police officer is killed by one man in the group. Saxe and Powers go underground.

The FBI organizes a nationwide dragnet for the fugitives. The feds invade women's groups and sweep through lesbian communities in Hartford, New Haven and around the country with a newly sharpened tool-- the Grand Jury.

Originally developed in old English law as a shield against arbitrary action by the king, grand juries are being used today by the government against political activists in over thirty political cases across the nation.

If you are called to testify, whether or not you know anything about fugitives, you cannot refuse to answer a prosecutor's questions. This gives the government full license to collect information on all activists and movements, whether or not they have any connection to illegal activity.

William Kunstler, famed radical defense attorney, comes to Connecticut and tells the public that grand juries are used by prosecutors as "tools" to strip citizens of their rights. "They are running wild over this country," Kunstler says.

In Connecticut, women activists find this out the hard way. Ellen Grusse, Terry Turgeon, Diana Perkins and Marianne Palmer are subpoenaed in March,1975 by the prosecutor, but refuse to talk to a New Haven grand jury. Perkins eventually provides limited testimony; Palmer's case is dismissed. The legal action sends a chill through feminist and lesbian organizing efforts.

"They are being sent to jail, not for failing to give information about the fugitives," charges radical Hartford attorney Mike Graham, "and not for committing any crime, but for refusing to divulge the names of their own friends and groups to which they belonged."

Ellen Grusse and Terry Turgeon initially spend 28 days in jail for refusing to cooperate with the feds.

The two women and their lawyers are pretty sure the FBI is bugging their phones. The feds insist they are not. (In 1977, a local newspaper reveals that 3,000 Connecticut residents have been wiretapped since 1970 in the course of a Black Panther trial. Over one thousand of them are later awarded damages by a court.)

Grusse and Turgeon are recalled to the grand jury in 1975 and once again refuse to name names. "We don't want to go to prison, but we will," Grusse says. They spend seven months in the Niantic State Prison, the length of the grand jury's operation. The National Council of Churches files a friend-of-the-court brief supporting the pair's fight against abuse of the grand jury system.

After five years on the run, Susan Saxe is arrested in Philadelphia, when a bank security camera photo surfaces showing her cashing a check in Torrington. Saxe eventually pleads guilty, with the proviso that she will not have to testify about any other person. She serves eight years in prison. In 1993 Katherine

Powers turns herself in after 23 years underground and is incarcerated for six years.

Not one National Guardsman or police officer is convicted of the deaths of the unarmed Kent or Jackson students. No army or government official is prosecuted for war crimes in southeast Asia.

Terry Turgeon and Ellen Grusse are released from prison on December 20, 1975. Their courage and principles have proven stronger than the federal government's threats.

Two months later, grassroots activists and progressive lawyers in Connecticut organize the "Committee to Defend Our Democratic Liberties" which opposes grand jury abuses and the new push by President Ronald Reagan to consolidate and ratchet up the federal criminal code in order to repress labor rights, quash the free press, and curb the right to privacy.

Unwelcome Guests at Senator Dodd's Office
November 29, 1984

"I don't like these sorts of things," mutters Senator Chris Dodd's state director. "It's unsettling."

He is referring to the ten members of the Atlantic Life Community who have taken over the U.S. Senator's office on 60 Washington Street. The sit-in is a "nonviolent response to the horrors of the times we live in," explains John Bach. The group demands that Dodd speak out forcefully against the bloody Central American wars that are being funded by the United States.

"It would certainly be nice if you leave before we leave," says a Dodd staffer. "Stanley, we invite you to join us," replies activist Art Laffin. Stanley calls the police instead and the activists are arrested. They are found guilty; three refuse to pay a fine and choose 30 days in jail.

This is not the first congressional sit-in, nor the last. On November 10, 1999, four anti-war protesters enter Senator Joseph Lieberman's office to discuss the deadly U.S. economic sanctions against Iraq. He refuses to meet with them. They remain in the office, ringing a bell every 12 minutes to signify the death of another Iraqi child caused by the sanctions.

Vieques Supporters say "Ni Una Bomba Mas "
June 27, 2001

Every bomb dropped on the practice range further spreads the poison, says a group of seven people who gather in front of the U.S. Armed Forces Recruitment Center in Hartford. They are here to protest the United States Navy's ongoing bombing and military training on the island of Vieques, Puerto Rico.

State Representative Evelyn Mantilla is one of the demonstrators arrested for the peaceful civil blockade at the military office on Pearl Street. The disobedient ones include members of the Green

In front of the Army recruitment office
(Thornton)

Party and Catholic Worker, along with a social worker, a grad student, and a Vietnam veteran.

The peacefully assembled group has engaged in this act of civil disobedience in an effort to call on President George W. Bush to fulfill his moral duty as Commander in Chief to respond to serious violations of human rights. Organized by the *Comité Todo Connecticut con Vieques*, protesters demand that the Navy must immediately end all military activities on the Island.

While the group is arrested when they block the entrance to the recruitment office, more than 100 supporters chant and demonstrate their support. Several prominent religious and political leaders show their support from the sidewalk on the other side of the street.

For 61 years, the people of the Puerto Rican municipality of Vieques have been subjected to the expropriation of their lands, forced migration and expatriation, bombings, and the destruction of the island's economy, natural resources and environment, all at the hands of the United States Navy.

The U.S. government denies the impact of the bombing practices in Vieques, and justifies its actions as essential to the U.S. national security. Yet, while the U.S. Navy's presence and practices have destroyed the island's key industries (fishing, agriculture, and cattle-ranching), the Navy employs only 30 of the island's 9400 local residents. Today, there exists an unemployment rate of almost 50%, and 72% of the island residents live below the poverty level.

More startling is that the children of Vieques are born, and its people live, under the shadow of preventable, painful and deadly diseases. For over sixty years, Navy bombings have produced toxic levels of lead and cadmium contamination.

The Navy's admitted use of tons of explosives, uranium shells, and napalm has led to an island-wide cancer rate which exceeds that of the Puerto Rico's main island by 27%, according to the Puerto Rican Department of Health.

Protests have been organized in Hartford and around the country since 1977 at the request of the Vieques Fishermen's Association. Momentum sags for a period but it is revived when David Sanes Rodriguez, a civilian guard, is killed in 1999 by an errant bomb.

A protest camp is set up near the military base. Thousands come to the island in solidarity with the residents. High-profile union leaders, elected officials and celebrities are arrested when they refuse to abandon their blockade of the base entrance.

These actions, including the Hartford arrests, continue for three more years.

Finally, the Bush administration announces that on May 1, 2003, all Vieques bombing will be terminated. Not one more bomb.

Tail Gunner Joe Can't Take the Heat
April 1, 2007

U.S. Senator Joseph Lieberman has served more than 40 years as a Connecticut politician. His popularity erodes over time, particularly for his uncritical support of U.S. war policy in the Middle East during the first two Gulf Wars.

The Senator runs for Vice President with Al Gore in his 2000 presidential bid. Like Gore, Lieberman does not protest the theft of the election by George Bush Jr. and facilitated by the U.S. Supreme Court.

Ultimately, he is challenged by progressive forces during the 2006 Democratic Party convention but wins the Senate nomination over newcomer and anti-war candidate Ned Lamont. Lieberman later loses to Lamont in an August primary. It is an astonishing blow to the man and the moribund political party satisfied with a "sure thing."

Lieberman runs that November for Senate as an independent Democrat. He wins the election with the support of Republican voters and the old guard of Connecticut, including State AFL-CIO president John Olsen, who also serves-- at the same time-- as the head of the state Democratic Party. Many more union activists actually oppose Lieberman and have been working for Lamont.

By this time, Lieberman his earned the nickname "Tail Gunner Joe," which refers to his chicken hawk status. The moniker was first given to Senator Joe McCarthy (D) of Wisconsin, a rabid anti-communist famous for leading witch hunts against liberal opponents and gay people in the military and the state department.

Lieberman's disappointing return to the Senate does not stop his opponents from continuing to pressure him for his hawkish, conservative positions. In 2001 students are pepper-sprayed in front of his Hartford office; in 2009 they sit-in and are arrested at his Washington office. They picket his Connecticut home as well.

Some activists despair that their actions are not having any effect, but soon Lieberman starts looking for a new home at 900 Chapel Street in New Haven. He figures that a high rise condo will keep protesters at a distance.

He confides as much to a building superintendent. "Picketing at my house, that's too personal," he says, admitting that the constant pressure is indeed having the desired impact

What Lieberman doesn't know is that the super is an active union member. Tail Gunner Joe's off-guard comment spreads quickly through the progressive community.

Pickets follow Lieberman to his new condo on April 1, 2007 to condemn his support for President George W. Bush and the escalation of the Iraq War--after Lieberman had won re-election promising to pull out U.S. troops.

Rabbi Israel Stein of Congregation Rodolph Shalom in Bridgeport is one of the demonstrators at Lieberman's home. Rabbi Stein, who had been a military chaplain in Vietnam, tells the crowd that each Saturday he reads the names of the war dead to his congregation.

"They sit there stunned as I read a dozen, two, sometimes three dozen names. That's my real *parsha*, my [Torah] chapter of the week. My congregants know, and we want Senator Lieberman to know, that each of these people is a boy or a girl who was not allowed by you, Senator, to grow up, to grow old, and to die in their bed. It can't go on. I want a storm of protest to grow and race across the country, as it did in the time of Vietnam, and this is part of it!"

Once again Lieberman moves-- this time to Stamford. There he is met by 500 angry protesters who expose his pro-insurance company stand against health care reform.

Human Rights

Inmates Strike at Seyms Street Jail
August 9, 1967

Instead of returning to their cells for the night, 145 inmates at Hartford's Seyms Street jail have organized a nonviolent sit down strike. They're fed up with the poor treatment and living conditions in the 1873-built facility sometimes called the "hell hole."

Committee Against Police Repression march and rally, 1976
(Homefront)

At 10:00 pm on August 9, 1967, the inmates, all from the maximum security ward, take their stand. Authorities call out the Hartford police, who surround the jail; state police are put on alert. The head of the jail rushes in from his suburban home.

Overcrowding, poor food, lack of medical care, and abuse by guards are among the 20 complaints the prisoners deliver to the jail authorities. Eventually they negotiate with a committee of corrections officials, a state senator and a newspaper reporter on these and other problems: lack of access to bail bondsmen and legal documents, restricted visitor privileges, jail job segregation, and no opportunity to exercise.

Five hundred men live in a building meant to house about 350. They are allowed one shower a week with no way to buy toilet paper, towels, soap or toothbrushes. There is no running water in the cells. Sometimes they get no drinking water from the guards. Lice, roaches, and rats move about undisturbed.

Solitary confinement can be made indefinite at the whim of a guard, the inmates say. They are stripped naked when they enter what is called "the hole," and have to urinate and defecate on the floor because there are no toilets, not even slop buckets.

The negotiations halt for the night, and after they are guaranteed no reprisals, the inmates end their brief strike at around 2:30 in the morning. The next day state officials tour the facility; some call the conditions "appalling" as they view soiled mattresses and smell the unwashed inmates.

The visitors meet David Bradshaw, 22 years old and already a civil rights veteran from his voter registration efforts in the south. David says he was picked up during the recent disturbances in

Hartford's north end. When he arrived at Seyms Street he was immediately put in "Siberia," a section of the jail worse than the rest.

Jail authorities promise some immediate improvements. They say other changes can only be made with more state funding.

Seyms Street has been the target of criticism since 1920, and the subject of a legislative investigation in 1938, but very little changes from year to year. In the course of its existence at least 75 men escape from the jail; too many have committed suicide there.

Although funds have been approved by the General Assembly to build a new jail, no suburban town will take it. The jail continues to be the site of protests by local community activists and college students who demand reforms to the "sub-human" conditions (in the words of a former corrections official).

Four years after the Hartford jail strike, the Attica prison uprising in September, 1971 becomes the most well-known jail rebellion in U.S. history. Refusal by New York Governor Nelson Rockefeller to meet directly with inmates over their grievances-- many similar to those of the Seyms Street strikers-- leads to an armed raid by authorities and many deaths.

Seyms Street is finally closed in 1977. Two inmates have recently committed suicide there. Prisoners are transported to the new Hartford Correctional facility on Weston Street.

Gay Power, from Stonewall to Hartford
September 3, 1971

Hartford's first gay liberation group decides that 'coming out' means direct action and if necessary, confrontation with the police.

On September 3, 1971, eleven Kalos Society members are arrested while protesting at a local gay bar where lesbians are being harassed by the management. The owners of the Park West club want women customers to dress "properly." They eject those who ignore the gender norm of the day.

Kalos Society event on Union Place
(courtesy of Richard Nelson)

Undeterred by the busts, Kalos members keep up their nightly pickets until the owner capitulates.

The Kalos Society formed in 1968 as a social organization (known as Project H) with the support of Episcopal Canon Clinton Jones. One of their early public events is a picnic outing at Goodwin Park in September, 1970 in spite of neighbors' protests.

The group quickly becomes the local "gay liberation front" inspired by the Stonewall Rebellion in New York, a militant 1969 response to constant police raids. Gay advocacy, which has mostly been quiet lobbying, has now taken on a public and assertive social justice quality.

Kalos publishes a regular newsletter, *The Griffin,* which is available at gay bars and in the stores at Hartford's Union Place (known for radical and counterculture activity). The group relates to politics of the left: the *Griffin* quotes Black Panther leader Huey Newton and sponsors a bus to a Vietnam war protest in Washington, D.C.

Less than a month after the bar protests, Connecticut becomes the second state in the nation to decriminalize private sexual relations between consenting adults.

ADAPT Sledgehammers Make a Big Impression
March 7, 1988

You're in a wheelchair and need to take a trip. How do you get to the bus or train? You can't ride over the stone curb to the station, and the lone access point is poorly identified.

Some disability-rights activists have a solution: to reach their destination, they will make their own "curb cuts." It's a DIY thing.

The activists are led by Clayton Jones, who is fresh off a protest against the inaccessibility of the so-called "Skywalk" that connects the Civic Center

Creative conversion of Union Place. Clayton Jones on right.
(Homefront archives)

with City Place. It's one of many public spaces
wheelchairs aren't welcome.

Americans Disabled for Access to Public
Transportation (ADAPT) has been using dramatic
direct actions across the country to bring disability
discrimination into focus. In Hartford, they have
chained themselves to Greyhound bus tires because
the company won't permit motorized wheelchairs
on board.

Now, with each heavy sledgehammer blow, the
activists start to transform the Union Station curb.
Police quickly arrest four of the demonstrators for
criminal mischief.

The arrestees refuse bail and choose to spend the
night in jail-- another headache for the authorities
who can't figure how to attend to the group's special needs.

Today, when you see a bicycle, baby carriage,
grocery cart, person with a cane, or in a wheel-

chair, successfully navigating a Hartford street, thank ADAPT.

The Squatters of People's Housing Action
July 14, 1988

With 3 million homeless people nationwide, and a housing vacancy rate of almost zero in Hartford, People's Housing Action forms to sharpen public focus on this basic human right.

Starting with a two day, 28-mile walk from Willimantic to Hartford, protesters communicate the cold, hard facts. "Five thousand people are on Section 8 waiting list in Harford," says Elna Moberg of the local YWCA's women's shelter. "These people are the working poor, unemployed, women and children," she tells a crowd of more than one hundred at Betances Park, the march's destination.

Section 8 is the federal housing subsidy program that eases, but does not cure, the city's housing crisis. A national study shows that nearly 4 million low cost housing units are urgently needed. The figure has doubled since Ronald Reagan became president.

Juan Figueroa, a state representative first elected by People For Change (PFC), the local third political party, tells the audience that three developers have bought nearly the entire housing stock on Park Street between Main and Hudson. He plans to meet the speculators to make sure they are not just building condos. "We don't need more dispersement" of families, Figueroa says.

On the evening of July 14, 1988, People's Housing Action helps to ratchet up the pressure. In Washington, D.C. there's a federal affordable housing act that will create 7.5 million new housing units that working people can afford.

In 60 cities around the nation, groups are occupying unused buildings that could be affordable housing sites as a way to bring attention to the federal bill.

The events have been inspired by Mitch Snyder and the Community for Creative Non-Violence (CCNV), which has spearheaded direct action support for the homeless in Washington. In 1984 Snyder went on a hunger strike until Reagan was forced to hand over a building that was sheltering hundreds of homeless people. The next year, Snyder was in Connecticut at a local college campus speaking on "Militarism and Hunger: the Connections."

Tonight's action is called "Take Off the Boards," and on Hudson Street, that's just what a dozen activists do. With crowbars and hammers they rip down the plywood that had been covering the doors and windows of 363 Hudson Street. The building was previously the site rented by PFC a few years back during its first successful election campaign. The third party had made affordable housing a top priority. Now, members of the group are part of the Hudson Street occupation.

One of those wielding a crowbar is Steve Sononne, a housing activist suffering from serious physical disabilities. Steve is also homeless. When asked by a reporter if he and his compatriots are planning to stay the night, Steve says yes. "I'll do what I always do, just grab a space on the floor."

The action has plenty of support throughout the city. Next store to the site, a second story window opens and out pops Ramon Quiros, the veteran community and civil rights activist. He is excited and happy to see what is transpiring. After a hearty pledge of support, Quiros flies the Puerto Rican flag out his window.

Taking Down the Boards. Steve Sononne (left),
John Bach with crowbar.
(Homefront archives)

The People's Housing Action squatters settle in for the night. By dawn, they are mildly surprised that neither the absentee landlord nor the police have made a move to evict them. Time for Plan B.

They walk three miles to Scarborough Street, on the posh side of town. In a stroke of very good luck, the rag tag bunch startles Congresswoman Barbara Kennelly as she is leaving her well-appointed home with a clutch of aides.

Will she support the federal affordable housing initiative in the U.S. House? Will she put her name on the bill? Yes, she replies, clearly anxious to get away from the group. As it turns out, Kennelly is en route to a press conference where she will announce her plans to return to Congress.

Four months later, on November 8th, Kennelly wins her re-election. Steve Sonnone and others are in D.C. ending a seven-week fast to spur more federal action on homelessness. He has lost forty pounds and is dangerously weakened. Is the fast worth it? Sononne replies: "We made the effort, and history will record the results."

Save Our Homeless People
April 12, 1990

Thirteen men and women have occupied a large room on the second floor of Hartford City Hall. It's not a purely symbolic action. Most of them are homeless. Even their church shelter has closed. There is no effective city policy for the growing homeless crisis. They plan to make to make the spacious public building their new home.

As it does each year, the Immaculate Conception men's shelter on Park Street announces it will close for the summer. Hartford City Councilwoman Sandi Little sends a volunteer from her group, People For Change (PFC), to an emergency meeting on the issue. If the shelter closes, where will the men go? The city's other shelters are full. The PFC staffer tells them the story of Isabel Blake, the welfare mom who organized a tent city on the State Capitol lawn nearly twenty years earlier. Some of the men remember Ms. Blake.

The housing crisis is nationwide in scope. For a decade Hartford has failed to create a policy to provide decent, long-term affordable housing and a short-term plan for the homeless. In fact, some members of the City Council-- particularly Deputy Mayor I. Charles Mathews-- are openly hostile to creating a workable homeless policy.

From the emergency meeting arises Save Our Homeless People Association (SOHPA), run by and for men who had been staying at the shelter. They are determined to face the local lawmakers.

On April 12th, just a few days after SOHPA's formation, the men and their supporters are in front of City Hall. Without proper shelter, "we will be living in the streets and in doorways," says Mario Mendes, a SOHPA leader. Summer time is even more dangerous for them than winter, since muggings increase when the homeless men live outside in the warm weather.

The thirteen set up camp inside the seat of the people's government. Councilman Mathews is furious. He wants to personally arrest two of the PFC volunteers (the cop in charge tells the fuming politician he can't). The men have barely settled in when the Hartford police move them to new living quarters: the local jail.

First protest at City Hall
(Homefront archives)

This is just the first step for SOHPA. The group travels to East Hartford to demand they stop dumping homeless people across the Hartford border. They win their free speech rights at Council meetings despite punitive threats from a shelter manager. They picket Deputy Mayor Mathews' Hartford home, where they suspect he doesn't really live. They hold a public wake for four comrades who died outdoors in the past year.

Forty Days, One Million Dead
August 6, 2001

"People are so impressed when they learn we are on a 40-day hunger fast to protest the U.N. sanctions against Iraq," says Hartford's Brian Kavanaugh. "But I tell them that here, at least, we have clean water to drink. The Iraqi people don't even have that. We will go back to relative prosperity, good food. But every six minutes an Iraqi child dies from malnutrition and preventable disease. And none of this has to be."

It's a hot August morning and Brian is on the 17th day of his fast. He and nine other people from around the country are standing across from the United Nations in New York, settled in right near the building that houses the United States Mission to the U.N. Brian is a member of the St. Martin de Porres Catholic Worker community on Clark Street in Hartford.

The U.N.-sponsored economic sanctions are enforced by the military might of the United States.

After a decade of this silent war against the people of Iraq, unemployment is over 60%, and more than two-thirds of the country's industry is defunct. Sanctions mean the basic chemicals needed to purify water cannot be imported. According to the U.N.'s own statistics, 5,000 children under five years old die each month as a result of the embargo. Read that again: 5,000 children die each month.

As a banner on the sidewalk proclaims: "Weapons of Mass Destruction: Nuclear Bomb, Hiroshima, August 6 1945, 140,000 civilians killed. Sanctions on Iraq, August 6, 2001, 1,000,000 civilians killed."

The ten people on this fast are not martyrs. In fact, they have called, written, faxed, and e-mailed the U.S. mission in an attempt to engage the officials in a dialogue about our government's support for the sanctions. The activists have prepared a typical meal that Iraqis are forced to live on: rice, lentils, flat bread, and a bottle of water from New York's East River--as clean as the water the Iraqis now drink. If the U.S. bureaucrats will meet and eat the meal with them, the ten women and men will break their fast.

In response, a U.S. mission spokeswoman says "we don't like to be threatened."

Smoking Out the Corporate Giant
April 25, 2012

The Hartford-based insurance company Cigna has been awarded between $50 and $70 million in state funds as a bribe to keep about 200 jobs in the state. "Giving money to Cigna is like giving away the candy store. It does nothing for Connecticut," says one angry protester who has spent the day at the State Capitol lobbying for better healthcare access.

Citizens challenge Cigna corporation
(courtesy of Healthcare4All)

Rising costs and a generous state subsidy are only part of what makes consumers angry. Cigna is very good at increasing profits by minimizing benefits. The company admits as much to shareholders at its annual meeting in Hartford's Bushnell Hall.

While the stockholders are inside, they can hear the chanting, singing and drumbeats of hundreds of angry citizens outside.

Despite a previous request, a dozen of them attempt to walk into the building and attend the meeting but are stopped by a large police contingent. The activists are arrested.

Meantime, the Rev. Damaris Whittaker and two other activists have successfully gotten inside the exclusive event. They each hold a few company shares, secured by friendly labor unions, which allow them to grill Cigna CEO David Cordani (who receives $40 million in annual compensation). They are the only ones in the room who ask Cordani anything at all about Cigna's responsibility to its customers, or to those who have been denied insurance pre-existing health conditions.

Inside the meeting, Union electrician and consumer activist John Murphy is told that "while low utilization of medical resources is a cause of large profits this year, it's not company policy."

Citizen lobbying, shareholder activism, public protest, and civil disobedience all combine to force the greedy insurance company out in the open. "It's an effective day's work," observes one of those arrested.

Immigrants Welcome Here
August 21, 2018

There have been hundreds of vigils and demonstrations in front of the Ribicoff federal building since its construction in 1963. Anti-war protests, gay rights rallies, political prisoner picket lines and other events have drawn faithful activists to a variety of worthy causes. The structure connects ordinary Hartford people, at least symbolically, to oppressive government policies.

But today, Salma Sikandar and her family stand

outside the federal building-- which houses the Immigration and Customs Enforcement (ICE) office-- waiting for the decision on her deportation to Bangladesh.

On Tuesday, August 21st, her supporters pitch tents on the sidewalk; ten people, led by Salma's husband Anwar, initiate a hunger strike. They are all determined to stay until Thursday at 9:00 am, the day set for Salma to surrender herself to ICE. The electronic shackle on her ankle ensures she won't attempt to evade the authorities.

Salma has lived in the U.S. for 18 years. She overstayed her visa and began applying for an extension in 2011. Her son Samir is just about to start his freshman year at Quinnipiac College.

A few weeks previously, thirty people were arrested in an attempt to block access to the Hartford ICE office. Donald Trump's racist immigration policies are separating hundreds of families and deporting thousands more.

In Connecticut, Trump's actions are overwhelm-

Immigrants Are Welcome Here: Camping
out at the Federal building (Thornton)

ingly unpopular. More than 43,000 people have signed a support petition for Salma in a few days. The Governor, U.S. congress members, and local officials express sympathy. Even her Republican state representative has defended Salma against local opposition.

Hartford is a city of immigrants; the Mayor and police department do not take action against the campers and hunger strikers despite federal requests to clear them out. The city changed its Municipal Code ten years ago, on July 23, 2008, making Hartford a sanctuary city. Municipal social and medical services cannot be restricted based on immigration status. City employees are not allowed to ask or disclose information on such status. Police are forbidden to ask about or detain a resident solely on the basis of status. Police are also forbidden to assist ICE enforce administrative warrants.

The direct action is a sign of the strength of Salma's statewide support base, especially the activists on the ground.

Twenty hours into the hunger strike they learn that ICE has granted her a stay of deportation. Says her husband: "Now she's still here, so that's all we need. We need to fight. And we're going to win this fight."

They pack up their tents and banners. Many are traveling to New Haven where another immigrant has sought sanctuary in a local church.

Samir, Salma and Anwar's son, prepares to start the new college semester.

Students

Refusing to Hide from Nuclear War
May 3, 1960

The Cold War has produced an arms race between the U.S. and U.S.S.R which now threatens worldwide nuclear destruction. As a response, the government requires all citizens to participate in "Civil Defense" drills. These futile efforts, which include racing to underground shelters or climbing under school desks, are meant to reassure the population that survival is possible.

Eleven college students from Wesleyan University and Hartford College for Women disagree. When the air raid sirens blast through the city, they take the only possible sane action – they picket in front of the State Capitol.

An earlier protest of 500 New Yorkers ended in 27 arrests and five days in jail. The Hartford police don't arrest these students but take down their names. The students' signs read "Civil Defense Breeds Militarism" and "There is Still Time, Brother."

One year later on April 28, 1961, protesters refuse to obey the air raid siren and picket on Main

Street, outside of the Old State House which has been designated as a nuclear shelter. Unlike the students in front of the Capitol, these young people are arrested and charged with obstructing Civil Defense functions. Nationwide, protests against nuclear proliferation grow.

Trinity College Sit-In Gets the Goods
April 24, 1968

In the early hours of the morning, weary students from Trinity College leave the administration building they have occupied over three days.

They leave with a signed agreement providing scholarships for potential Black students. The agreement guarantees $15,000 for the coming year ($104,000 in today's dollars).

Dean Roy Heath and Trinity College President Albert C. Jacobs are forced to negotiate with the 150 students who have taken over the Williams Building, where most administration offices are located. The action has been timed to coincide with the school's Board of Trustees meeting. The Trinity Association for Negroes is in the lead, and student Terry Jacobs, president of TAN, plays a key role in the occupation.

The action begins on the afternoon of April 22nd. The trustees and two administrators are "held captive" by the students or four hours, the College charges.

Trinity Sit-in Ends, Funds Promised

Discipline Faces Top Protestors

By THEODORE DRISCOLL

Student occupation of Trinity College's administration building ended early this morning with agreement by the college to match a $15,000 student fund for "scholarships for the culturally disadvantaged."

The accord came at about 12:30 a.m. today's and followed a student sit-in at Williams Memorial, which houses most of the college's administration offices, since late Monday afternoon.

About 150 demonstrating students stayed in the building all Monday night.

Dean Roy Heath said that Terry Jones, head of Trinity Assn. of Negroes, and five other demonstration leaders would be charged with holding the trustees and two administrators captive for four hours Monday. He said the matter would be decided "internally." The students will appear before the Student-Faculty Disciplinary Committee and the outcome could range exoneration to expulsion, he said.

Signed by Jacobs

The statement of agreement was signed by Trinity College President Dr. Albert C. Jacobs and read by College Chaplain Alan Tull.

The statement said, "We can now commit $15,000 with the intention to go as far beyond that as the budget of the college will allow."

The administration negotiators also said the college "will admit as many qualified Negro students as are available and will provide adequate financial aid for them . . .

"We agree that the college should guarantee a minimum of 15 full scholarships for disadvantaged students this year."

Chaplain Tull avoided calling the college's agreement a concession to the students' demands. "We should not talk of concessions now that we have reached agreement," he said.

Deadlock

Roy Heath, dean of Trinity College, meets with students Tuesday afternoon after a recess in negotiations over Negro scholarships between demonstrators and a college committee representing the trustees. The negotiators met in the college chapel for two hours and no agreement was reached. Heath told the students the meeting would reconvene at 9:30 p.m. (Courant Photo by Arthur J. Warmsley).

Trinity College Student Sit-inets the Goods (Homefront archives)

Now, after the agreement is settled and the students' demands are met, a College spokesman announces that six student leaders, including Terry Jacobs, will be charged, and face possible expulsion for holding the administrators against their will.

Practically all college campuses across the nation

have been challenged by the civil rights movement. Hartford's Black community has had active campaigns for housing, jobs, and quality education for a number of years. Activists point out that UConn, Connecticut's largest public university, has enrolled only a handful of black students in its history.

Trinity College is a private school, all male, which mostly caters to the "one-percent" of the economic elite and trains them to lead the country. One exception is Ralph Allen, a Trinity student from Massachusetts, who graduated in 1965. Two years earlier he was held in a Georgia jail without bond for months, on the charge of "insurrection." Allen was a field secretary for the Student Nonviolent Coordinating Committee (SNCC), who had taken time off from Trinity to organize voter registration. Charges were eventually dropped thanks to student protests and pressure on national politicians.

Now, in April 1968, this event at Trinity is special in its own way. The students' victory comes just twenty days after the assassination of Dr. Martin Luther King, Jr.. They have turned their outrage into disruptive-- and constructive-- action.

Students Teach their Elders About Free Press
February 21, 1969

It takes African American high school students to teach the Hartford establishment about the First Amendment.

88

Marcus Manselle, Weaver High senior and publisher of the student newspaper *The People's Press*, is first to report that faculty and students have begun a picketing campaign at the Chamber of Commerce on February 7, 1969. The Chamber has proposed that $3.5 million be cut from the Board of Education budget. The *Hartford Courant* has to rely on Manselle's report to figure out what's going on.

The underground newspaper is written and printed by Manselle, Louise Billie, and Cliff Hankton at their own expense. Distribution takes place on school property, without official approval. The city's lawyer rules that the paper is "hate literature," filled with "racist" and "obscene" material. In fact, the students are speaking out about their alienation, the lack of school relevance, and student rights.

The Weaver administration informs Manselle, Billie and Hankton that they must stop handing out the paper or suffer the consequences. They refuse. The Board of Education suspends the three on February 21st without bothering to engage them in a discussion. Manselle is forced into "home instruction" during his suspension. Even after the other two students are allowed to return to school, Manselle's suspension continues.

The newspaper does not stop publishing. It surfaces again in April with more support than ever: students, teachers, and the Ebony Businessmen's League all speak out for Manselle and criticize the suspensions. The 120-member Weaver Student Senate backs Manselle. The school's parents and alumni meet to support the cause, as do the local

Students Teach their Elders About Free Press; High School students march down Albany Avenue toward the Chamber of Commerce (Hartford History Center)

Black Panthers. The University of Hartford's student newspaper *UH News Liberated Press* follows the story, prints his essays, and puts Manselle on their staff list.

A state judge refuses to issue an injunction on Manselle's discipline, despite a 1968 U.S. Supreme Court decision that upholds free speech in schools (specifically, the right of Iowa students to wear black armbands in honor of Martin Luther King).

On May 1st, another issue of *The People's Press* is distributed on the Blue Hills Avenue sidewalk in front of Weaver. Students also leaflet in front of City Hall and ask Mayor Ann Uccello to support their fight. She says the issue is not within her jurisdiction. The Weaver Student Senate takes the controversy to the Board of Education, calling for Manselle's reinstatement and the establishment of a student court that can review and overturn disciplines.

On May 27, after being stonewalled by every city authority, 500 Weaver students go on strike for three days. Strikers urge those still in the classrooms to join them, and more students leave the school. Students march to the Board office on High Street. They attempt to enter a Board-faculty meeting but are refused entrance. "I want nothing more to do with you," says an exasperated board president Alfred Rogers.

The fight continues into June. Finally, with the help of NAACP president Wilber Smith, a working group of students, parents, school officials and Board members hammer out a resolution. The proposal allows on-campus distribution of independent student papers as long as they don't interfere with normal school business or "inflame or incite" students. Marcus Manselle's suspension continues, however, and he does not graduate with his class.

In 1976, Weaver High School becomes the Martin Luther King, Jr. elementary school. It was Dr. King, speaking at the Lincoln Memorial in 1963, who told the crowd "Somewhere I read of the freedom of press. Somewhere I read that the greatness of America is the right to protest for right."

General Student Strike
May 5, 1970

Nixon bombs Cambodia. National Guardsmen kill four students at Kent State University. Police kill two teenagers and wound more at a Jackson State protest (the Mississippi students were organizing against the Vietnam War, the Kent State killings, and local racist conditions).

Hundreds of thousands of college and high

school students, including those at dozens of Connecticut schools, respond with a general strike in May, 1970. One hundred students sit in at Governor John Dempsey's office until he agrees to meet with him.

During one mass march in Hartford, at least 1,000 protesters take to the highway and stop traffic.

Across the country students occupy university buildings and clog the streets against a war that is already nine years old and will continue until the last U.S. troops are evacuated in 1975. Unprecedented acts of mass civil disobedience, including G.I.s who refuse orders they believe to be illegal and immoral, culminate a year later on May 5, 1971 in Washington, D.C. There, the May Day Tribe shuts down much of the capitol city, resulting in the arrest of 13,500 activists.

Decades later, their arrests and incarceration at RFK Stadium are deemed to have been illegal, and thousands of protesters are offered restitution. The May Day actions become a template for future mass occupations, including the Clamshell Alliance convergence on the site of the New Hampshire Seabrook nuclear plant (1977), the Wall Street Action against corporate profits from nukes (1979), Occupy Wall Street (2011), and the Standing Rock water protectors in North Dakota (2016). Hartford people take part in all of these actions.

Bibliography

Good Writing on Nonviolent Direct Action

"Many Roads to Morning: Rethinking Nonviolence," from Webs of Power - Notes from the Global Uprising, by Starhawk http://bit.ly/Starhawkrethink

Handbook for Nonviolent Campaigns, 2nd Ed., (English or Spanish), for purchase or free download, War Resisters International, http://www.wri-irg.org/pubs/NonviolenceHandbook

Revolution and Equilibrium, Barbara Deming

How We Win: A Guide to Nonviolent Direct Action Campaigning, George Lakey

A Force More Powerful: A Century of Non-violent Conflict, Peter Ackerman, Jack DuVall (also a documentary film)

A Dolores Huerta Reader, Mario T. García

Mahatma Gandhi and His Myths: Civil Disobedience, Nonviolence, and Satyagraha in the Real World, Mark Shepard

Freedom's Daughters: The Unsung Heroines of the Civil Rights Movement from 1830 to 1970, Lynne Olson

This Is an Uprising: How Nonviolent Revolt Is Shaping the Twenty-First Century, Mark Engler and Paul Engler

Challenging Authority: How Ordinary People Change America, Frances Fox Piven

Nonviolence in America: A Documentary History, Staughton Lynd and Alice Lynd, editors

"Why Black Bloc Tactics Won't Build a Successful Movement," Waging Nonviolence

http://wagingnonviolence.org/feature/why-black-bloc-wont-build-successful-movement/

Books by Gene Sharp:

Sharp's Dictionary of Power and Struggle: Language of Civil Resistance in Conflicts

Waging Nonviolent Struggle: 20th Century Practice And 21st Century Potential

Politics of Nonviolent Action, Three volumes (Power and Struggle, Methods, Dynamics)

I Warned You: Books that argue against Nonviolent Direct Action

This Nonviolent Stuff'll Get You Killed: How Guns Made the Civil Rights Movement Possible, Charles E. Cobb

The Failure of Nonviolence, Peter Gelderloos

Pacifism as Pathology, Ward Churchill

About the Author

About the author: Arrest at Plastonics Strike, 1990 (Nick Lacy)

Steve Thornton is the creator of The Shoeleather History Project, which documents and explores stories from Hartford's grassroots. He maintains a website, leads workshops, and conducts interactive walking tours that feature ordinary people who are the real makers of history. Steve has been an activist and organizer all his life and retired in 2013 as a vice president of District 1199/SEIU, Connecticut's largest healthcare union.

In his capacity as an educator, Steve has engaged more than 3,000 rank and file healthcare workers to become workplace leaders through popular education. He has also trained hundreds of people from Vermont to Georgia in civil disobedience/nonviolent direct action. He regularly speaks to students ranging from elementary schools to universities, as well as to historical societies, union picket lines, and activist groups.

Steve has written for a variety of publications including Connecticut Explored, Hartford Courant, Industrial Worker, Labor Notes, Justice (ILGWU), Hartford Business Journal, Hartford News, The Guardian (U.S. radical newsweekly), Z Magazine, CT Mirror, ConnecticutHistory.com, and LAWCHA Labor Online.

He is the author of Wicked Hartford (The History Press, 2017) and A Shoeleather History of the Wobblies: Stories of the Industrial Workers of the World (IWW) in Connecticut (Red Sun Press 2013). Steve appears in three documentary films, America: From Hitler to MX (1983), Bloodletting (2004), and Crossing the American Crises (2011). His organizing work is featured in Social Movements and Activists in the USA by Stephen Valocchi. He is a proud husband, father, and grandfather.

TITLES FROM HARD BALL PRESS

A Great Vision: A Militant Family's Journey Through the Twentieth Century, Richard March

Caring: 1199 Nursing Home Workers Tell Their Story, Tim Sheard, ed.

Fight For Your Long Day, Classroom Edition, by Alex Kudera

I Still Can't Fly: Confessions of a Lifelong Troublemaker, Kevin John Carroll (Winter 2018-19)

Love Dies – A Thriller, Timothy Sheard

The Man Who Fell From the Sky – Bill Fletcher Jr.

Murder of a Post Office Manager – A Legal Thriller, Paul Felton

New York Hustle: Pool Rooms, School Rooms and Street Corner, A Memoir, Stan Maron

Passion's Pride: Return to the Dawning – Cathie Wright- Lewis

The Secrets of the Snow –Poetry, Hiva Panahi

Sixteen Tons – A Novel, Kevin Corley

Throw Out the Water – Sequel to Sixteen Tons, Kevin Corley

We Are One: Stories of Work, Life & Love – Elizabeth Gottieb, ed.

What Did You Learn at Work Today? The Forbidden Lessons of Labor Education, Helena Worthen

With Our Loving Hands: 1199 Nursing Home Workers Tell Their Story, Timothy Sheard, ed.

Winning Richmond: How a Progressive Alliance Won City Hall, Gayle McLaughlin

Woman Missing – A Mill Town Mystery, Linda Nordquist

The Lenny Moss Mysteries – Timothy Sheard

This Won't Hurt A Bit
Some Cuts Never Heal
A Race Against Death
No Place To Be Sick
Slim To None
A Bitter Pill
Someone Has To Die

CHILDREN'S BOOKS from HARD BALL PRESS

Joelito's Big Decision, La gran Decisión de Joelito:
Ann Berlak (Author), Daniel Camacho (Illustrator),
José Antonio Galloso (Translator)
Manny and the Mango Tree, Many y el Árbol de Mango:
Alí R. and Valerie Bustamante (Authors), Monica
Lunot-Kuker (Illustrator). Mauricio Niebla
(Translator)
The Cabbage That Came Back, El Repollo que Volvió
Stephen Pearl & Rafael Pearl (Authors), Rafael Pearl
(Illustrator), Sara Pearl (Translator)
Hats Off For Gabbie, ¡Aplausos para Gaby!:
Marivir Montebon (Author), Yana Murashko (Illus-
trator), Mauricio Niebla (Translator)
Margarito's Forest/El Bosque de Don Margarito:
Andy Carter (Author), Alison Havens (Illustrator),
Sergio Villatoro (Graphic Design),
Artwork contributions by the children of the Saq Ja'
elementary school
K'iche tranlations by Eduardo Elas and Manuel
Hernandez
Translated by Omar Mejia

Jimmy's Carwash Adventure, La Aventura de Jaime en el Autolavado:
Victor Narro (Author), Yana Murashko (Illustrator), Madelin Arroyo (Translator)
Good Guy Jake/Buen Chico Jake,
Mark Torres (author), Yana Murashko (illustrator), Madelin Arroyo (translator)
Polar Bear Pete's Ice Is Melting!
Timothy Sheard (author), Kayla Fils-Aime (illustrator), Madelin Arroyo (translator)

HOW TO ORDER BOOKS:

Order books from www.hardballpress.com, Amazon.com, or independent booksellers everywhere.
Receive a 20% discount for orders of 10 or more, a 40% discount for orders of 50 or more when ordering from www.hardballpress.com.